ONTOLOGICAL INTEGRATION

Salman A. Nensi

ONTOLOGICAL INTEGRATION

Salman A. Nensi

Zariqa
www.zariqa.com

Table of Contents

Introduction

We live in a world where impressions, good and bad, are made in a fraction of a second, and effective communication is vital in order to deliver your message to the right people. Following is a list of Nensi's insights and immediate recommendations, which he believes can do much to enhance an organisation's ability to communicate globally and better achieve its ultimate goals.

Priority #1:
Capacity Assessment

Every organisation can benefit from a full capacity assessment of its present communications and marketing systems—hardware, software, organisational systems and personnel—across the whole spectrum of levels, branches, committees, assemblies, etc. For this, the organisation should take the following steps:

1) Determine what it possesses in terms of communications and marketing systems resources and how those resources are currently being used.

- How are the current marketing vehicles conceived and managed?
- Is anyone in charge of overseeing the stickiness of the organisation's websites?
- Is anyone doing "blue sky" thinking that might lead to new and interesting ideas, such as attending a local book fair to help get the organisation's message out?
- Why were these marketing vehicles created?
- Who is the audience?
- What is the desired effect?
- How successful are these marketing vehicles, and were success indicators assigned prior to the campaign (money, column inches, sticky web hits, etc.)?

2) Cross-reference this information with other systems used in the past (e.g., solid marketing, communications and information-sharing systems—"lessons learned" that the organisation can utilize).

3) Pull all this information into ONE online, easily accessible database of:

- communications capacity;
- availability of that capacity to others in the organization; and
- systems to access this capacity acrossthe organization.

4) Determine how to provide more support for communications and information technology personnel through the process of capacity building.

A capacity assessment will provide the information your organisation needs to move forward. Once you know what has or has not worked in the past, and what tools and communication strategies the organisation is currently using, it becomes possible to adjust these methods and increase reach, and effectiveness.

Benefits

- A group, team, committee or agency anywhere in the organisation that needs communications assistance will **save time and money almost instantly**.
- It is also well documented that requesting input from long-term staff **significantly boosts morale** and is of far more interest to workers than the amount of their financial raise each year.
  - Example: A client learned which existing staff member could help with a web project using capacity assessment. The project was done in 48 hours and cost only two days of human resource time instead of the USD $20,000 budgeted for the project.

Priority #2:
Capacity Building—Internal Messaging

Every organization can benefit from a proper, professionally trained, well-funded communications staff, plus teams that work together internally to push the many messages of the many parts of the organization to its many audiences (see Priority #3). Capacity building ensures that your current staff is used as efficiently as possible, so external costs are avoided. The organization should use the capacity assessment to inform a capacity building plan that includes the following steps:

1) Create well-defined, detailed job descriptions and easy-to-understand-and-use communications systems. The plan should remove ambiguity and clarify work processes. A six-page memo on how to write an email is overkill.

2) Identify holes and weak points in hardware, software, and personnel capacity, and address them.

3) Design internal communications and marketing vehicles that are culturally sensitive, and prioritize clear and efficient communication.

4) Build an online, comprehensive communications course specific to the organization's needs, in multiple languages if necessary, to make sure all existing communications and information management staff are at the same base level. This course will:

- be practical rather than theoretical, easy to use and understand, and of high quality;
- be able to grow and change over time, taking on new ideas and adding local tweaks where logical and useful;

- feature solid help files; and
- potentially incorporate material already available. For example, the Canadian Broadcasting Corporation's *The Age of Persuasion*, a 30-minute weekly lay-person's show on marketing and how it operates in our world, could be used as part of the training, rather than expending resources to create new materials.

Nensi provides capacity building globally in many areas of marketing and communications and specialize in media management training. He also provides capacity building in print and web design, photography, event design and planning, as well as in marketing and communications plan generation.

It is important to remember that simply owning a digital camera does not make you a photographer, and writing weekly memos to your boss does not make you a good and effective writer. A true professional is able to set the stage, contextualize the material, and connect the dots for the stakeholders, conveying the message clearly and effectively.

- Marketing is **not only** about making a newsletter.
- Communications is **not only** about crisis management.
- Translation is **not only** about using a dictionary.
- Photography is **not only** about pointing and clicking.
- Public relations is **not only** about making phone calls.
- Editing is **not only** about correcting spelling.
- Print design is **not only** about choosing colours.
- Web design is **not only** about adding links and pictures.
- Project management is **not only** about telling people what to do.

Benefits

- **Save time and money** by training existing personnel to a base level of communications proficiency.
- **Boost morale yet again**, because studies show that staff who know what they need to do and are well-trained with good tools are far more productive and happier at their jobs.
- **Increase the quality, reach and effectiveness** of communications messages.
- **Weed out** institutionalized bad communications habits.
- **Make adaptation faster and easier** for communications personnel new to the environment.

Priority #3:
Sales and Marketing—Outbound Messaging

Every organization can benefit from a proper sales and marketing plan. It is sometimes difficult for organizations to think of themselves as needing to "sell" and "market" what they do, but in this fast-moving universe, your message must be clear and striking enough to grab the viewers' attention and hold it. In order to design a proper plan, your organization must identify to whom you are selling what message, how you are selling it, and most importantly, WHY.

How does an organization acquire an effective sales and marketing plan?

1) Determine what needs to be communicated and to whom.

- Stakeholders need education about how communications and marketing projects work, how to properly monitor and evaluate a communications project, and whom to contact within the organization for information.
- People want to know what the organization does.
- Connect with **pro**sumers instead of just **con**sumers.

2) Use capacity assessment (see Priority #1) to evaluate the full range of marketing and communications vehicles currently used by the organization.

3) Use a capacity building plan to capitalize on the resources that are available in the organization.

4) Based on the above analyses, modify current marketing strategies for maximum effectiveness. Design the plan to take

into account all the component parts of the organization and the fact that each has a communications goal and agenda.

Nensi has decades of experience selling and marketing products, from fast-moving consumer goods to arts and cultural products. He has worked for NGOs, arts organizations, governments, ministries, and others who are selling ideas and concepts rather than units. Nensi is experienced in creating all types of marketing vehicles, from traditional print-based to broadcast to new technologies, as well as multiformat and multiplatform campaigns. He is able to assist with everything from small projects that need finishing to larger ideas that need conceptualizing.

Benefits

- **More buy-in** on what the organization is doing.
- **More understanding** from customers about the organization.
- **More goodwill** from customers.
- **More organizational unity.**

Priority #4:
Ontology

Every organization can benefit from an ontology strategist to coordinate capacity assessment and capacity building. Nensi sees ontology as more than the technical patches that allow old computer systems to talk to each other; ontology is the framework that allows the individuals and groups within an organization to communicate among themselves and with the IT department. This builds technological and personnel-based synergies, harmonies, and integrations to ensure the organization's various messages are delivered to the appropriate internal and external stakeholders.

In order to achieve these synergies, the organization must do the following:

1) Use the capacity assessment and the capacity building plan to build and fix communications from within, utilizing existing resources.

2) Use existing systems of communication and add emerging technologies of the new network economy rather than building new and costly custom solutions from scratch.

3) Utilize current staff, systems, personnel, etc., as much as possible.

4) Bring IT and communications staff together to work in a meaningful way. Encourage IT to use their knowledge base to help solve technical communications issues. Help communications staff keep IT from getting clogged up with redundant systems work.

This collectively is called semantic integration and enterprise application integration—both of which are possible with the proper coordination of existing communications and information technology capacity. Full integration of hardware, software, systems of organization, suppliers and both the creators and recipients of messages will improve efficiency and ensure that the needs of all the stakeholders are met.

Benefits

- A proper communications system will **save money from every budget** and **save time for every person** working at the organization by significantly reducing duplicate workloads and effort spent searching for data/information.
- Even more significantly, this savings will allow **more of both time and money to be used for productive works** rather than for administration.
- Having a clear order of operations for fulfilling the organization's goals will **significantly improve morale** as shared goals are attained, setting the tone for **more and greater collective achievement**.
- A unified delivery system will allow the organization's message to flow freely within the organization, among donors, clients, and the general public, through channels such as the web, print, and broadcast both locally and worldwide, thereby **reducing stress on overtaxed systems**.

Some Ideas and Tools

Get the organization's systems and funding up to speed:

- There are 1,000 billionaires on the planet; they should be tapped.
- There are approximately 30 large tech firms on the planet; they should be tapped.
- What is the intellectual rights and properties situation at the organization? Can consumer and media products be created to help extend the brand and message while earning some funds?

Get the organization's story out:

- A magazine (online, print, broadcast; NOT a newsletter)
- A reality TV show (This sounds a bit far-fetched but it really is not. There are multiple ways of organizing a show and that would create tons of spin-offs.)
- A celebratory publication (Pick a future anniversary; hook the book and global marketing on it.)
- A website featuring those who have made significant contributions to the organization

Conclusion

Imagine how a unified and streamlined communications system can reduce levels of stress, confusion, misinformation, misapprehension, misallocation, and misdirection. Imagine how such a system will increase morale, efficiency, and accuracy, while freeing up time and funds for the organization, its staff and the work they do.

Salman A. Nensi
International Communications Manager
www.Nensi.com

Zariqa
Est. 2021